written by Jay Dale

illustrated by Amanda Gulliver

Lea wanted a rabbit.

"No! No! No!" said Dad.
"You can't have a rabbit!"

"Oh, Dad!" said Lea.
"Why not?
I'll take good care of it."

"We have nowhere to put it," said Dad.

"You could make a hutch," said Lea.

"I don't have time," said Dad.

"A rabbit is only little," said Lea.
"It will not take long
to make a little hutch.
Oh, please, Dad!
Please! Please! Please!"

"Will you take care of it all by yourself and feed it every day?" asked Dad.

"Yes!" said Lea. "I will."

"Will you clean its hutch and put in fresh straw?" said Dad.

"Yes!" said Lea. "I will."

"Well," said Dad, "I'll think about it."

"Oh, Dad," said Lea.

"Not now!" said Dad.
"I have to go to work
and you have to go to school.
We'll talk about this after school."

That afternoon, Lea tried again.

"Dad," said Lea,
"I'm going to tell you **why**
I would make a good pet owner."

So Lea got some paper and a pencil.

Dear Dad,

I will take good care
of my rabbit every day.

I will feed it morning and night.

I will give it fresh water every day.

I will clean out its hutch
and put in fresh straw.

I will hug my rabbit
and love it lots.

Love,

Lea

Dad read the letter.
"Mmmmm,"
he said.
"I'll think about it."

Just then, there was a knock at the door.

"Now who could that be?" asked Dad,
as he walked towards the door.

Lea peeked out the window.
She saw a lady getting into a little van.
Dad opened the door, and there on the
doorstep was a small cage.
Inside the cage was a little brown rabbit!

"Oh!" cried Lea, peeking around Dad's legs. "It's a rabbit!"

The rabbit was very tiny.
It had one ear that went up
and one ear that went down.

"Dad," asked Lea,
"is this rabbit for me?"

Dad just smiled.

"Look!" he said, as he opened the cage. "There's a letter inside."

As Dad started to read the letter, Lea picked up the rabbit and gave it a big hug.

Dear Lea

This rabbit is just for you.

Your dad told me you will take good care of it.

Love,

The Secret Bunny Fairy

xxx

Later that day, Lea smiled at Dad.
"I love my rabbit," she said.
"And I love you, too!"

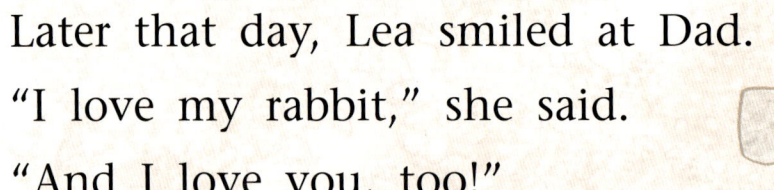